ADRIAN NEWEY

THE LIFE FROM BEGINNINGS TO END

By
FACT PUBLISHER

ADRIAN NEWEY HISTORY

Copyright © 2024 FACT PUBLISHER

All rights reserved.

No part of this publication may be reproduced, distributed, or transmitted in any form or by any means, including photocopying, recording, or other electronic or mechanical methods, without the prior written permission of the publisher, except as permitted by U.S. copyright law.

ADRIAN NEWEY HISTORY

TABLE OF CONTENTS

INTRODUCTION
CHAPTER ONE
THE EARLY YEARS
CHAPTER TWO
THE FORMATIVE YEARS
CHAPTER THREE
THE RISE TO PROMINENCE
CHAPTER 4
THE WILLIAMS ERA
CHAPTER FIVE
THE MCLAREN INNOVATIONS
CHAPTER SIX
RED BULL RACING AND THE NEWEY LEGACY
CHAPTER SEVEN
BEYOND THE RACETRACK
CHAPTER EIGHT
THE ENGINEER'S MIND
CHAPTER NINE
THE FINAL LAP
CHAPTER TEN
REFLECTIONS AND FUTURE HORIZONS
EPILOGUE
THE AUTHOR'S CLOSING THOUGHTS ON ADRIAN NEWEY'S LIFE AND CAREER.
CONCLUSION

ADRIAN NEWEY HISTORY

INTRODUCTION

In the high-octane world of Formula One, where the roar of engines is only matched by the thunderous applause of millions, one mind has consistently outpaced the competition. Adrian Newey, the mastermind behind some of the most successful racing cars in history, has not just shaped the contours of vehicles but has also carved the future of motorsport with his visionary designs.

This biography unveils the man behind the drafting table, the genius in the pit lane, and the legend whose life is a blueprint of relentless pursuit of perfection. From his early days sketching car designs as a child to revolutionising the racetrack with aerodynamic marvels, Newey's journey is a testament to the power of innovation and the spirit of engineering.

ADRIAN NEWEY HISTORY

Embark on a narrative that accelerates through the corners of Newey's personal and professional life, exploring the depths of his passion and the peaks of his achievements. This is not just a story of a man who designs cars; it's the chronicle of a creator who has repeatedly defied the limits of speed and success.

Prepare to be riveted by the tale of a living legend, whose legacy is etched not in trophies, but in the very fabric of Formula One itself. Adrian Newey: the man who dreams in horsepower and thinks in aerodynamics. Your journey through his life starts now.

An overview of Adrian Newey's impact on Formula One and motorsports.

Adrian Newey's influence on Formula One and motorsports is nothing short of revolutionary. His innovative car designs, aerodynamic expertise, and meticulous attention to detail have significantly impacted the sport, often introducing groundbreaking concepts that prompted governing bodies to change regulations to maintain competitive balance.

Newey's career in Formula One has been marked by a series of pioneering achievements that have set new standards in racing car performance.

His work ethic is characterised by an unceasing drive to refine details and improve performance, illustrating his commitment to excellence in Formula One engineering.
Over the years, Newey has consistently pioneered new ways to enhance racing cars, setting a high standard for other teams in the sport.

At Williams and McLaren in the 1990s, and then at Red Bull over the last 15 years, Newey built 14 championship-winning cars. His vision and brilliance have helped Red Bull Racing to become a dominant force in the sport, contributing to their 13 titles in 20 seasons.

ADRIAN NEWEY HISTORY

His exceptional ability to conceptualise beyond F1 and bring wider inspiration to bear on the design of grand prix cars, his remarkable talent for embracing change, and his relentless will to win have been pivotal in Red Bull Racing's success.

Newey's departure from Red Bull is described as 'seismic' for F1, underscoring the major influence he has had on the racing team and the sport as a whole. His legacy will continue to echo through the halls of Milton Keynes, and the RB17 Track Car will be a fitting testament to his time with Red Bull Racing.

In summary, Adrian Newey's impact on Formula One and motorsports can be seen in the numerous championships his designs have won, the innovative approaches he has brought to car design, and the lasting legacy he leaves as he moves on to new challenges.

ADRIAN NEWEY HISTORY

His career is a testament to the power of innovation and the spirit of engineering in the world of high-speed racing.

CHAPTER ONE

THE EARLY YEARS

Adrian Newey's genesis in the world of motorsport engineering was as remarkable as the trajectory his career would later take.

Born on a winter's day in Stratford-upon-Avon, the same town that gave the world Shakespeare, Newey's early life was steeped in the pastoral beauty of Warwickshire, England. His father, a veterinarian, and his mother, a wartime ambulance driver, provided a nurturing environment for young Adrian, whose fascination with the mechanics of motion began early.

The halls of Repton School, an institution with a legacy of academic rigour, became the crucible where Newey's intellect was forged. It was here, among peers like motoring journalist Jeremy Clarkson, that his penchant for pushing boundaries emerged.

ADRIAN NEWEY HISTORY

A rebellious spirit coupled with a passion for sound led to an infamous incident involving the school's stained glass windows and the band Greenslade's amplifiers, a testament to his desire to test limits.

Despite being asked to leave Repton, Newey's academic prowess was undeniable. His journey continued at the University of Southampton, where he pursued aeronautics and astronautics, disciplines that marry the science of air and space.

It was here that Newey's talent soared, culminating in a first-class honours degree a harbinger of the extraordinary designs he would later bring to the racetracks.

Upon graduation, the world of motorsport welcomed Newey with open arms. His first foray into this high-speed realm was with the Fittipaldi Formula One team, where he worked under the tutelage of Harvey Postlethwaite. The March team soon beckoned, offering him a role that would set the stage for his future successes.

In these formative years, Newey's designs did not merely occupy the physical world; they were the embodiment of his relentless quest for aerodynamic perfection.

His creations in the IndyCar circuit, particularly the March 85C, not only clinched championships but also etched his name in the annals of racing history.

Thus, the early years of Adrian Newey's life were a blend of rebellion, intellectual brilliance, and an unquenchable thirst for innovation. These elements coalesced to form the foundation of a career that would revolutionise the world of Formula One, leaving an indelible mark on the sport and on the very concept of speed itself.

ADRIAN NEWEY HISTORY

BIRTH AND FAMILY BACKGROUND.

Adrian Newey's story begins in the historic town of Stratford-upon-Avon, Warwickshire, England, where he was born on December 26, 1958. His entry into the world coincided with the cold embrace of winter, yet his life would be anything but cold, as he would go on to ignite the fiery passion of motorsports with his innovative designs.

The son of Richard and Edwina Newey, Adrian was born into a family where professional dedication and service were the norm. His father, a veterinarian, instilled in him a meticulous attention to detail and a respect for the precision of science.

His mother, who served as an ambulance driver during the tumultuous times of World War II, undoubtedly influenced Adrian with her resilience and ability to navigate through life's most challenging moments.

ADRIAN NEWEY HISTORY

This blend of precision and resilience would become the hallmark of Newey's career. The seeds of his future successes were sown in a household that valued hard work, ingenuity, and the courage to push boundaries.

These values, coupled with the rich cultural heritage of his birthplace, provided a fertile ground for the young Newey to cultivate his dreams.

As a child, Adrian's imagination was captivated by the mechanics of movement and the thrill of speed. This fascination laid the foundation for a lifetime of innovation, leading him to a path where his creations would one day dance with the winds of racetracks around the world.

In the tapestry of Formula One history, the threads of Newey's family background are woven tightly into the fabric of his achievements. His lineage is not merely a footnote in his biography but a prologue to the story of a man whose designs would revolutionise the sport of racing.

EDUCATION AND EARLY INFLUENCES

Adrian Newey's educational journey and early influences are a testament to his unyielding pursuit of excellence and a prelude to his legendary status in the world of motorsport engineering.

His academic odyssey began at Repton School, where he shared corridors with future motoring journalist Jeremy Clarkson. However, his time at Repton was cut short by a rebellious act that shattered not just the school's windows but also the conventional expectations of a student's path.

This expulsion did not deter Newey; rather, it fueled his determination to succeed on his own terms. He redirected his focus to the University of

Southampton, where he immersed himself in the study of aeronautics and astronautics.

It was here that Newey's passion for engineering took flight, culminating in a first-class honours degree that heralded the beginning of an illustrious career.

The early influences that shaped Newey's approach to design were as varied as they were profound. From the intricate mechanics of model aeroplanes to the adrenaline-fueled world of motorcycle racing, each experience honed his understanding of aerodynamics and the delicate balance between form and function.

These formative years were not merely a prelude to his professional achievements but the very crucible in which his design philosophy was forged.

Upon graduation, Newey's talents were quickly recognized by the motorsport industry. He began his career with the Fittipaldi Formula One team, working under the guidance of Harvey Postlethwaite.

It was a pivotal moment, as Newey transitioned from student to engineer, from theory to application. The March team soon recognized his potential, bringing him on board and setting the stage for the innovations that would redefine racing car design.

Thus, Adrian Newey's education and early influences were characterised by a blend of intellectual rigour, creative rebellion, and a relentless quest for knowledge. These elements combined to create a designer whose work would not only win races but also inspire generations of engineers to come.

CHAPTER TWO

THE FORMATIVE YEARS

The formative years of Adrian Newey, a name synonymous with the zenith of motorsport engineering, are a narrative of ambition, precision, and the relentless pursuit of aerodynamic excellence.

His journey, which began in the quaint town of Stratford-upon-Avon, took a pivotal turn at the University of Southampton, where the young prodigy pursued a degree in Aeronautics and Astronautics. It was here, amidst the hallowed halls of academia, that Newey's passion for racing and his innate understanding of aerodynamics coalesced into a singular focus.

Graduating with first-class honours, Newey's academic achievements were a mere prelude to the feats of engineering he would soon accomplish. His early career was marked by a series of astute moves, each one a stepping stone towards his eventual dominance in Formula One design.

The Fittipaldi Formula One team became his first professional proving ground, where under the mentorship of Harvey Postlethwaite, Newey's talents began to flourish.

The March team, recognizing his potential, soon enlisted his skills. It was here that Newey's designs first tasted the thrill of competition, his creations gracing the European Formula 2 circuits.

The experience was invaluable, honing his skills not just as a designer but also as a race engineer, a dual role that would become a hallmark of his career.

These formative years were not merely a time of learning and growth for Newey; they were the forge in which his design philosophy was tempered.

ADRIAN NEWEY HISTORY

The principles he established during this period of innovation, meticulous attention to detail, and a relentless pursuit of performance would become the cornerstones of his future successes, propelling him to the forefront of motorsport engineering.

UNIVERSITY DAYS AND FIRST CLASS HONOURS DEGREE IN AERONAUTICS AND ASTRONAUTICS

Adrian Newey's university days at the University of Southampton were a period of profound intellectual growth and the sharpening of a mind that would one day engineer victories at the pinnacle of motorsport.

In the late 1970s, Southampton's halls of learning became the crucible where Newey's innate talent for understanding the physics of airflow and mechanical design was honed academically.

His pursuit of a degree in Aeronautics and Astronautics was not merely academic; it was a passionate quest to grasp the very elements that, when mastered, could propel machines to victory.

The culmination of his studies was marked by the achievement of a first-class honours degree in 1980, a testament to his exceptional grasp of the complex interplay between aerodynamic forces and engineering principles. This academic accolade was not just a piece of paper; it was a launchpad that propelled Newey into the stratosphere of motorsport engineering.

Those university years were also a time of inspiration and ideation for Newey. The theories and principles he absorbed would later translate into the sinuous curves and aggressive lines of championship-winning Formula One cars.

It was at Southampton that Newey's vision began to take shape, a vision that would eventually redefine the aesthetics and mechanics of high-speed competition.

In those formative years, Newey was not just a student of engineering; he was an artist in the making, learning to sculpt the wind itself into a tangible advantage on the racetrack.

His first-class honours degree was a mere prologue to the storied career that awaited him, a career that would be characterised by an unyielding drive to innovate and a relentless pursuit of perfection.

EARLY CAREER MOVES AND ENTRY INTO MOTORSPORTS.

Adrian Newey's early career moves and his foray into the world of powersports are a narrative of ambition, precision, and a relentless pursuit of aerodynamic perfection. Upon graduating with a first-class honours degree in Aeronautics and Astronautics from the University of Southampton in 1980, Newey's path was clear.

ADRIAN NEWEY HISTORY

His academic prowess was not just a testament to his understanding of engineering principles but also a beacon that guided him towards the echelons of motorsport engineering.

Newey's entry into motorsports was swift and decisive. He began his career with the Fittipaldi Formula One team, working under the esteemed Harvey Postlethwaite.

This experience was crucial, as it provided Newey with a firsthand look at the pinnacle of motorsport competition and the complexities of Formula One engineering.

In 1981, Newey's journey took a significant turn when he joined the March team. Here, he transitioned from a race engineer for Johnny Cecotto in European Formula 2 to designing racing cars.

It was a period of profound growth and learning, where Newey's designs began to take shape and his potential as a motorsport engineer started to be realised.

These early career moves were not just steps on a ladder for Newey; they were leaps towards a future where his designs would dominate the racetracks of the world.

His entry into motorsports was the beginning of a legacy that would see his creations clinch victories and championships, forever changing the landscape of Formula One racing.

CHAPTER THREE

THE RISE TO PROMINENCE

Adrian Newey's ascent to the pinnacle of motorsport design is a tale of relentless innovation and an unyielding drive to redefine the boundaries of speed. His rise to prominence began with a fusion of his academic brilliance and his early career experiences, which laid the groundwork for his future successes.

In the crucible of Formula One, where every millisecond counts and every design decision can mean the difference between victory and defeat, Newey emerged as a visionary. His tenure at Williams in the early 1990s marked the beginning of an era of dominance.

ADRIAN NEWEY HISTORY

The cars he designed were not mere machines; they were masterpieces of engineering that blended form and function in ways previously unimagined.

Newey's designs during this period were characterised by their innovative use of aerodynamics, which allowed Williams to surge to the forefront of the sport.

The team's success was not just a testament to Newey's genius but also to his ability to work synergistically with the drivers and the rest of the engineering team to extract every ounce of performance from the car.

The cars that bore Newey's signature during this golden era were more than just vehicles; they were the embodiment of his design philosophy. They were a statement that in the world of Formula One, innovation was the key to success, and Newey was its master craftsman.

As Newey's reputation grew, so did the legend of his designs. Each team he graced with his presence became a force to be reckoned with, and his departure often left a void that was difficult to fill.

His ability to understand and exploit the intricacies of Formula One regulations became his trademark, allowing him to stay ahead of the curve and his competitors.

Newey's rise to prominence in the world of motorsport design is a narrative that transcends the sport itself. It is a story of a man whose passion for engineering and design has left an indelible mark on Formula One, shaping its history and defining its future.

TRANSITION TO FORMULA ONE

Adrian Newey's transition to Formula One was a pivotal moment in his career, marking the beginning

ADRIAN NEWEY HISTORY

of a legacy that would forever alter the landscape of motorsport engineering.

His journey to the zenith of racing began with his tenure at the Fittipaldi Formula One team, where he first dipped his toes into the complex and competitive world of F1 engineering.

The year was 1980, and the world of Formula One was on the cusp of a technological revolution. Newey, fresh from his academic triumphs, found himself amidst the roar of engines and the smell of burning rubber, a stark contrast to the quiet halls of Southampton.

It was here, under the guidance of Harvey Postlethwaite, that Newey began to translate his theoretical knowledge into practical, race-winning solutions.

His move to the March team soon after was where Newey's potential began to crystallise. As he designed racing cars for the European Formula 2 circuits, his creations quickly gained recognition for their innovative aerodynamics and performance on the track.

This period was not just about learning the ropes; it was about challenging the status quo and pushing the boundaries of what was possible in car design.

With each passing season, Newey's reputation grew, and it wasn't long before his name became synonymous with cutting-edge design and aerodynamic efficiency.

His transition to Formula One was not just a step up; it was a leap into a realm where his designs would battle against the best in the world, etching his name into the annals of motorsport history.

NOTABLE EARLY DESIGNS AND CONTRIBUTIONS

Adrian Newey's early designs and contributions to the world of motorsport engineering are a testament to his genius and a prelude to the storied career that would follow.

His tenure at March Engineering was the crucible where his talent for design and his understanding of aerodynamics melded to produce racing cars that would leave an indelible mark on the tracks.

Newey's first notable success came with the March GTP sports car, which dominated the IMSA's GTP class in 1983 and 1984. This early triumph was a harbinger of the success that would become synonymous with Newey's career.

His foray into IndyCar racing further cemented his reputation as a designer par excellence. The March 85C, an IndyCar project, not only won the CART Championship but also claimed victory at the prestigious Indy 500 racing series in 1985.

These early designs were not just vehicles for competition; they were bold statements of Newey's design philosophy. Each car was a blend of form and function, embodying Newey's relentless pursuit of aerodynamic efficiency and his ability to push the boundaries of existing technology.

The impact of Newey's contributions during these formative years of his career extended beyond the victories on the track. They laid the groundwork for a new era in motorsport design, one where innovation and a deep understanding of aerodynamics would become the cornerstones of success. Newey's early designs and contributions were the first chapters in what would become a legendary career in Formula One engineering.

CHAPTER 4

THE WILLIAMS ERA

The Williams era stands as a monumental chapter in Adrian Newey's illustrious career, a period where his genius for design and innovation propelled the team to the zenith of Formula One.

It was during this epoch that Newey's prowess truly shone, crafting machines that were not merely cars but symphonies of speed, precision, and aerodynamic beauty.

In 1990, Newey's arrival at Williams marked the genesis of what would become a golden age for the team. The initial season laid the groundwork, setting the stage for a series of triumphs that would redefine the sport. By 1991, the team had ascended to second place in both constructors' and drivers' championships, a prelude to the dominance that was to unfold.

ADRIAN NEWEY HISTORY

The year 1992 heralded the dawn of Williams' supremacy, with Newey's FW14B becoming an icon of F1 engineering. The car, driven by Nigel Mansell, roared to victory, clinching both the constructors' and drivers' championships. Mansell's teammate, Riccardo Patrese, followed closely in second, solidifying their dominance with an impressive ten wins out of sixteen races.

The following year, the team's relentless pursuit of excellence continued unabated. The FW15C, another masterpiece from Newey's drafting table, carried Alain Prost to his fourth and final drivers' title, with Damon Hill finishing third. The team once again secured the constructors' championship, a testament to their unbroken spirit and Newey's design acumen.

Newey's tenure at Williams was not just about creating winning cars; it was about pushing the envelope of what was possible within the sport's regulations. His designs during this era were a fusion of art and science, each car a canvas where Newey painted with the wind, sculpting airflows that would lead his drivers to glory.

The Williams era, therefore, is not merely a collection of seasons or a tally of victories; it is the story of a man whose vision transcended the racetrack, whose designs became the standard by which all others were measured, and whose legacy within the sport remains unparalleled.

ACHIEVEMENTS WITH WILLIAMS F1.

Adrian Newey's tenure at Williams F1 is etched in the annals of Formula One as a time of unparalleled success and innovation. His arrival at Williams in 1990 heralded the beginning of a golden era for the team, where his designs would not only dominate the racetrack but also redefine the very essence of racing car design.

ADRIAN NEWEY HISTORY

The Williams FW14B, a masterpiece of Newey's ingenuity, became the chariot of choice for Nigel Mansell, who, under its wings, soared to an astounding nine race wins in the 1992 season.

This vehicle was not just a car; it was a marvel of technology, equipped with active suspensions that maintained a constant ride height, maximising downforce and leaving competitors in its wake.

In 1993, the Williams FW15C, another brainchild of Newey, carried Alain Prost to his fourth and final drivers' title. The car was a technological titan on wheels, boasting advancements such as ABS, fly-by-wire systems, and traction control. It was a testament to Newey's vision that the FW15C was considered one of the most technically advanced F1 cars ever made.

Under Newey's guidance, Williams clinched five constructors' titles, a feat that stands as a tribute to his profound understanding of aerodynamics and mechanical design.

Drivers like Mansell, Prost, Damon Hill, and Jacques Villeneuve became world champions, piloting Newey's creations to glory and etching their names, alongside his, into the fabric of Formula One history.

The Williams era, therefore, is a narrative of triumph, a saga of a man whose designs transcended the realm of imagination and became the gold standard in the high-stakes world of Formula One racing.

THE DEATH OF AYRTON SENNA AND ITS IMPACT.

The tragic death of Ayrton Senna during the San Marino Grand Prix on May 1, 1994, is a sombre chapter in the annals of Formula One, a moment that reverberated through the sport and beyond.

For Adrian Newey, then the chief designer at Williams, the impact was profound and deeply personal. Senna, a racing icon, perished behind the wheel of a car born from Newey's drawing board, the Williams FW16.

The accident not only shook the foundations of Formula One but also prompted a period of introspection for Newey. The loss of Senna, a driver he had worked with closely, led him to question his future in the sport.

The burden of grief was compounded by a legal ordeal, as Newey, along with other members of the Williams team, faced charges of manslaughter in Italy, a process that would stretch out over several years before ultimately being acquitted.

Newey's reflections on the tragedy reveal a man grappling with the weight of responsibility. The incident forced him to confront the inherent dangers of motorsport and the role of a designer in safeguarding the lives of those who pilot their creations. It was a stark reminder that the quest for speed and success is invariably entwined with risk.

The aftermath of Senna's death saw sweeping changes in Formula One, with a renewed emphasis on safety that would lead to significant advancements in the protection of drivers. For Newey, the event was transformative, altering his approach to design and leaving an indelible mark on his philosophy.

The lessons learned from that fateful day in Imola continue to influence the sport, ensuring that Senna's legacy endures not just in memory, but in the very fabric of Formula One safety.

In the wake of tragedy, Newey emerged with a renewed sense of purpose, his designs reflecting a balance between performance and safety. The sport of Formula One, too, evolved, becoming a safer arena for the gladiators of the modern era.

The death of Ayrton Senna, and its profound impact on Adrian Newey, remains a poignant reminder of the fragility of life and the relentless pursuit of progress.

CHAPTER FIVE

THE MCLAREN INNOVATIONS

Adrian Newey's tenure at McLaren was a period marked by a relentless quest for innovation and a deep understanding of the intricate dance between aerodynamics and mechanical design.

His arrival at McLaren in 1998 was a pivotal moment, not just for the team but for the sport of Formula One as a whole. The MP4-13, the first car he designed for McLaren, was a testament to his ability to adapt and innovate within the rapidly evolving technical regulations of the sport.

The MP4-13 was a marvel of engineering, a single-seater that boasted a particularly compact design with a low centre of gravity, a feature that minimised the effects of load transfers.

This design philosophy was a direct response to the radical changes in regulations that demanded a narrower car width and the introduction of grooved tires.

Newey's innovations at McLaren were not limited to the MP4-13. His mastery of active suspension systems, which he had honed during his time at Williams, was further refined at McLaren.

The active suspension could be adjusted to make the diffuser stall in a straight line, a concept that Newey would later revive during his tenure at Red Bull Racing.

The genius of Newey's designs lay in his holistic understanding of the single-seater. He did not view the car merely on an aerodynamic level but possessed a profound knowledge of the mechanics at the level of transmission and suspensions.

ADRIAN NEWEY HISTORY

This unique quality allowed him to create cars that were not only aerodynamically efficient but also mechanically harmonious.

At McLaren, Newey's contributions went beyond the cars he designed; they extended to the very culture of innovation within the team. His approach to design and problem-solving inspired a generation of engineers and designers, fostering an environment where pushing the boundaries of technology was not just encouraged but expected.

The McLaren era, therefore, is a chapter in Newey's career that encapsulates his enduring legacy as one of the greatest ever car designers in Formula One.

His innovations during this period were not just solutions to the challenges posed by the sport's regulations; they were visionary leaps that propelled McLaren, and Formula One, into a new age of technological excellence.

KEY DEVELOPMENTS AND VICTORIES WITH MCLAREN.

Adrian Newey's era at McLaren is a testament to his enduring legacy as a master of innovation and a pivotal figure in the annals of Formula One. His tenure at the British team was marked by a series of key developments that not only showcased his design prowess but also led to significant victories that bolstered McLaren's standing in the sport.

The MP4-13, the first car designed by Newey for McLaren, was a revelation in the 1998 season. It was a machine that perfectly encapsulated Newey's philosophy of blending aerodynamic efficiency with mechanical harmony.

The car's compact design and low centre of gravity, coupled with a revolutionary approach to the newly introduced grooved tires, allowed McLaren to clinch the constructors' title and propelled Mika Häkkinen to his first drivers' championship.

ADRIAN NEWEY HISTORY

Newey's innovations at McLaren were not confined to a single season. The subsequent MP4-14 continued the winning streak, with Häkkinen defending his title in 1999. This car was a further evolution of Newey's design principles, pushing the boundaries of technology within the sport's stringent regulations.

Throughout his time at McLaren, Newey's designs were characterised by their cutting-edge aerodynamics and his ability to foresee and adapt to the changing tides of Formula One's technical landscape.

His contributions during this period were instrumental in securing McLaren's position as a formidable force in the sport, earning him accolades and solidifying his reputation as one of the greatest engineers in the history of Formula One.

The McLaren era, under Newey's technical leadership, was a symphony of speed and success, a period where every line drawn and every curve crafted on the drawing board translated into victories that echoed across racetracks around the world. It was a time when Newey's midas touch turned the aspirations of a team into the gold of trophies and the glory of championships.

CHAPTER SIX

RED BULL RACING AND THE NEWEY LEGACY

Adrian Newey's legacy at Red Bull Racing is a saga of relentless innovation, a narrative that intertwines his genius with the very essence of Formula One's evolution.

His tenure at Red Bull Racing, which began in 2006, marked the commencement of an era that would witness the team's meteoric rise to the pinnacle of motorsport excellence.

The RB3, Newey's first car for Red Bull Racing, was a harbinger of the transformation that lay ahead. Though it faced mechanical and reliability challenges, it was a solid step forward, laying the foundation for a future of dominance.

The subsequent seasons saw incremental improvements, but it was the comprehensive aerodynamic rule changes in 2009 that allowed Newey to showcase his design prowess. The RB5, born from these changes, was a triumph, securing six victories and catapulting the team to second in the Constructors' Championship.

The years that followed were a testament to Newey's mastery over the sport's technical intricacies. From 2010 to 2013, the team, under his technical guidance, achieved an unprecedented clean sweep of both the Drivers' and Constructors' Championships, with Sebastian Vettel clinching all four drivers' titles.

This period was marked by a staggering 41 winners' trophies and a total of 85 podium finishes.

Newey's brilliance extended beyond the racetrack. His return to focus on the RB16 was a strategic move to challenge the dominance of Mercedes.
The result was Max Verstappen's first Drivers' title in 2021, a crowning achievement that underscored Newey's enduring impact on the team's success.

As Newey prepares to step back from his Formula One design duties to focus on the final development of Red Bull's first hypercar, the RB17, his departure is not just the end of an era but the beginning of a legacy that will continue to inspire.

His vision and technical leadership have been instrumental in achieving a remarkable seven F1 Drivers' and six Constructors' Championship titles, totaling 118 victories and 101 poles.

Adrian Newey's story at Red Bull Racing is not merely a record of triumphs; it is a chronicle of a visionary who redefined the parameters of car design, a strategist who turned the tides of competition, and an innovator whose creations will forever echo in the annals of Formula One history.

JOINING RED BULL RACING

When Adrian Newey penned his name on the contract with Red Bull Racing in 2006, it was not merely a change of teams; it was the beginning of a revolution in Formula One. Newey, already established as a leading figure in motorsport engineering, brought to Red Bull Racing a vision that would elevate the team from mid-grid anonymity to the zenith of racing glory.

The union of Newey's design philosophy with Red Bull's ambition was a catalyst for change. The team, under his technical leadership, embarked on a rigorous development program that saw incremental but significant improvements.

Podium finishes became more frequent, and the team's competitiveness surged, setting the stage for a series of victories that would soon follow.

The 2009 season was a turning point. Comprehensive aerodynamic rule changes presented teams with a largely blank canvas, and Newey, with his unparalleled understanding of aerodynamics, seized the opportunity.

The RB5, his first car under the new regulations, was not just competitive; it was a harbinger of the dominance that Red Bull Racing would soon exert over the sport.

Newey's arrival at Red Bull Racing was a confluence of opportunity and expertise, a moment when the right person joined the right team at the right time.

His joining was a statement of intent, a declaration that Red Bull Racing was no longer content to be just another team on the grid. They were there to win, and with Newey at the helm, they had the means to do just that.

CONSECUTIVE FORMULA ONE CHAMPIONSHIPS

Adrian Newey's tenure at Red Bull Racing is a narrative of relentless pursuit and unparalleled

ADRIAN NEWEY HISTORY

success, a testament to his enduring legacy as a mastermind of Formula One engineering.

His arrival at the team in 2006 marked the beginning of a new chapter, not just for Red Bull but for the sport itself. The years that followed would see Newey's designs dominate the pinnacle of motorsport, achieving a feat that few could dream of: consecutive Formula One championships.

The crescendo of Newey's work with Red Bull Racing began to resonate across the F1 world in 2010. It was a symphony of innovation and performance that culminated in four consecutive constructors' and drivers' championships from 2010 to 2013.

These were years when the Red Bull cars, under Newey's technical direction, became the standard bearers of excellence. Sebastian Vettel, behind the wheel of Newey's creations, secured his place among the legends of the sport, clinching four drivers' titles in a row.

The legacy of these consecutive championships is not merely found in the trophy cabinets at Red Bull Racing's headquarters; it is etched in the very spirit of Formula One.

Newey's cars were marvels of aerodynamics and mechanical synergy, each component working in concert to deliver unrivalled performance on the track. The RB6, RB7, RB8, and RB9 were not just machines; they were the embodiment of Newey's vision, each victory a chapter in the story of his genius.

The impact of these consecutive championships reverberated beyond the circuits. They changed the landscape of Formula One, raising the bar for what was possible and inspiring a generation of engineers and designers.

Newey's influence extended to the regulations themselves, with his innovative designs often prompting changes to maintain competitive balance within the sport.

In the annals of Formula One, the era of Red Bull Racing's dominance under Adrian Newey's guidance will be remembered as a golden age, a time when the fusion of technical brilliance and competitive spirit wrote a saga of success that will inspire for generations to come.

THE DOMINANT RB19 AND ITS HISTORICAL SIGNIFICANCE

The Red Bull RB19, a masterpiece of Formula One engineering, is a testament to Adrian Newey's unparalleled design prowess. In the annals of motorsport, few cars have achieved the legendary status of the RB19, a vehicle that not only dominated the 2023 season but also redefined the parameters of racing excellence.

ADRIAN NEWEY HISTORY

Crafted under Newey's guidance, the RB19 was the culmination of years of innovation, a perfect storm of aerodynamic efficiency and mechanical precision.

The car's performance was nothing short of historic, as it carried Max Verstappen to an astonishing 19 grand prix victories in a single season.
This feat set a new benchmark for dominance in the sport, breaking records and cementing the RB19's place in the history books.

The RB19's success was not merely a result of incremental improvements but a radical reimagining of the car's aerodynamic potential. Built upon the foundation laid by its predecessor, the RB18, the RB19 was significantly lighter and added an unprecedented amount of downforce to an already perfect platform.

This allowed the car to maintain consistent downforce across all ride heights and conditions without succumbing to the proposing issues that plagued its competitors.

Newey's design philosophy, which has always placed a premium on the harmony between aerodynamics and suspension, was evident in the RB19.

The car's suspension system was designed to work in conjunction with the underfloor aerodynamics, a concept that Newey had mastered over his illustrious career.

This synergy allowed the RB19 to deliver a level of performance that was both awe-inspiring and seemingly effortless.

The RB19's historical significance extends beyond its record-breaking campaign. It represents the pinnacle of Newey's career, a design that not only won races but also pushed the boundaries of what was thought possible in the sport.

The car's dominance was a complete surprise even to Newey, who had anticipated that the second year of the ground effect aerodynamics era would see the competition close the gap.

In the end, the RB19 stands as a monument to Newey's genius, a car that will be remembered not just for its victories but for its contribution to the evolution of Formula One.

It is a vehicle that embodies the spirit of innovation that has driven Newey throughout his career, a spirit that continues to inspire and challenge the world of motorsport engineering.

CHAPTER SEVEN

BEYOND THE RACETRACK

Adrian Newey's influence extends far beyond the racetrack, his vision shaping not only the world of Formula One but also the broader realm of automotive design. His career, while rooted in the high-stakes arena of motorsport, has implications that reach into the future of road car technology and beyond.

Newey's expertise in aerodynamics and his relentless pursuit of performance have led to innovations that have trickled down from the exclusive domain of Formula One to the cars we drive every day.

Features like disc brakes, once a novel technology in racing, have become standard in modern vehicles, and materials such as carbon fibre, which

ADRIAN NEWEY HISTORY

Newey has extensively utilised in his race car designs, are increasingly finding their way into high-performance road cars.

But Newey's ambitions are not confined to the advancements of the past. His vision for the future is one where the symbiosis between F1 technology and road cars continues to evolve.

The hypercar project, the RB17, is a testament to this vision, where Newey's genius in design and aerodynamics will be applied to create a vehicle that promises to revolutionise the hypercar market.

As Newey prepares to step away from his Formula One duties, his focus shifts towards new horizons. The announcement of his departure from Red Bull Racing in early 2025 has sent ripples through the motorsport community.

His future endeavours, while not yet fully disclosed, are anticipated with great interest and excitement.

The prospect of Newey applying his design philosophy to new challenges and industries is a tantalising one, promising to bring about a new era of innovation and excellence.

Thus, Adrian Newey's legacy "Beyond the Racetrack" is one of a visionary who has not only shaped the world of motorsport but also stands poised to influence the future of automotive design and technology. His career is a narrative of relentless innovation, a journey that continues to inspire and challenge the boundaries of engineering and design.

PERSONAL MOTORSPORTS ACTIVITIES

Adrian Newey's personal motorsports activities reflect the same passion and precision that he brings to his professional endeavours. While known for his unparalleled success as a Formula One engineer, Newey's engagement with motorsport is not confined to the design office; he is also an active participant in racing, albeit in a more personal capacity.

His foray into the world of racing extends to taking the wheel himself. Newey has competed in various historic racing events, piloting classic cars with the same zeal with which he approaches car design.

These activities are not merely hobbies; they are extensions of his lifelong dedication to motorsport, providing him with a hands-on understanding of the vehicles he so masterfully crafts.

Newey's involvement in personal motorsport activities is a testament to his belief in experiencing the full spectrum of racing. It is one thing to design a car that can win championships; it is another to feel the car's power, balance, and behaviour on the track.

This firsthand experience undoubtedly feeds back into his work, giving him unique insights that only a driver-engineer could possess.

Through his personal engagement with racing, Newey bridges the gap between the theoretical and the practical, between the drawing board and the asphalt.

His presence on the track is a reminder that at the heart of every great designer is a racer, eager to push the limits, to feel the rush of speed, and to understand, on a visceral level, the machines they create.

FAMILY LIFE AND PERSONAL INTERESTS

Adrian Newey's life away from the drafting tables and pit lanes is as rich and multifaceted as the cars he designs. His personal life, marked by a deep commitment to family and a range of interests that span beyond the racetrack, paints the portrait of a man whose passions are as intricate as his engineering feats.

Married three times, Newey's family life is a tapestry woven with the threads of love, dedication, and the shared joy of his four children. His first marriage to Amanda in 1983 brought two daughters into his world, Charlotte and Hannah, before their paths diverged in 1989.

His second marriage to Marigold in 1992 welcomed his son Harrison and daughter Imogen, adding new hues to the family palette, though this union too would see its conclusion in 2010.

Beyond the confines of his professional achievements, Newey harbours a passion for the arts and history, interests that offer a respite from the relentless pace of Formula One.

His personal pursuits are reflective of a mind that seeks not only the thrill of competition but also the quiet contemplation offered by diverse cultural experiences.

Newey's personal interests extend to the skies as well. An avid enthusiast of aviation, his fascination with flight is not just limited to the aerodynamics of racing cars but also encompasses the broader realm of aircraft design and history. This passion for flight mirrors his professional life, where the principles of aerodynamics play a central role.

In essence, Adrian Newey's family life and personal interests provide a glimpse into the man behind the legend. They reveal a figure who, while renowned for his professional accomplishments, cherishes the quieter moments of life, the bonds of family, and the pursuit of knowledge and beauty in all its forms.

CHAPTER EIGHT

THE ENGINEER'S MIND

The engineer's mind is a realm where creativity intersects with precision, where art meets science. In the case of Adrian Newey, this confluence has produced some of the most iconic machines in the history of Formula One.

His mind, a crucible of innovation, has been the birthplace of designs that have not only won races but have also transformed the sport.

Newey's ability to visualise airflow and aerodynamic forces is akin to an artist visualising the strokes of their next masterpiece before the brush even touches the canvas.

This capacity to 'see' the invisible forces that dictate the behaviour of a racing car at high speeds is a rare gift, one that Newey has honed over decades of dedication to his craft.

ADRIAN NEWEY HISTORY

His approach to engineering is both intuitive and methodical, a duality that has defined his career. Newey's designs are not mere assemblages of metal and carbon fibre; they are intricate puzzles where every piece must fit perfectly, serving the dual gods of speed and safety.

His work is guided by an innate sense of how each component will interact with the whole, a holistic understanding that is the hallmark of his genius.

At the heart of Newey's success is his ability to marry the creative with the analytical. His background, with a father who had a keen interest in mathematics and engineering and a mother's family that was deeply artistic, provided the perfect genetic and environmental cocktail for nurturing a mind capable of groundbreaking engineering feats.

Newey's journey into the depths of engineering began in his youth, during long summer holidays spent sketching racing cars and turning those sketches into three-dimensional models.

This early practice in visualisation and design laid the foundation for his future successes, embedding in him the skills that would one day change the face of Formula One.

The engineer's mind, especially one as gifted as Newey's, is a treasure trove of potential. It is a place where the laws of physics are not constraints but challenges to be overcome, where every rule is an opportunity for innovation.

Newey's mind is where engineering becomes art, and where the cars that emerge from his drawing board become legends on the racetrack.

NEWEY'S DESIGN PHILOSOPHY AND APPROACH TO ENGINEERING CHALLENGES

Adrian Newey's design philosophy and approach to engineering challenges are the alchemy that turns raw technical potential into racing legend.

His philosophy is rooted in a deep understanding of aerodynamics, a field where he has been a pioneering force, shaping the contours of Formula One cars long before the full extent of its significance was recognized.

Newey's approach is characterised by an intuitive grasp of airflow, a skill honed through a lifetime of dedication to the craft of car design.

He possesses the rare ability to visualise the invisible, to see the air as it interacts with the car's surfaces, to understand how every curve, every angle, will affect performance.

This skill, he believes, is a blend of genetics and experience, a combination of his father's interest in mathematics and engineering and his mother's artistic lineage.

His career is a testament to the power of this blend, as he has consistently designed cars that not only perform but also inspire.
Newey's work is marked by a relentless pursuit of innovation, a willingness to push the boundaries of current technology, and an unyielding commitment to excellence.

His designs are not just solutions to the challenges posed by the sport's regulations; they are visionary leaps that propel teams to victory and redefine the sport itself.

Newey's approach to engineering challenges is holistic. He sees the car as a single, integrated entity where every component must work in harmony.

This perspective allows him to create designs that are both beautiful and effective, achieving a balance between form and function that is the hallmark of his cars.

In essence, Adrian Newey's design philosophy and approach to engineering challenges are about more than just winning races; they are about advancing the sport of Formula One, about creating cars that are as aesthetically pleasing as they are fast, and about inspiring the next generation of engineers and designers to dream bigger and reach further.

CHAPTER NINE

THE FINAL LAP

The final lap in Adrian Newey's illustrious career at Red Bull Racing is not merely a conclusion but a crescendo of a symphony that has played out over the course of two decades.

As the chief technical officer, Newey's departure in early 2025 marks the end of an era that has seen Red Bull Racing ascend to the zenith of Formula One, a period defined by innovation, triumph, and the relentless pursuit of perfection.

Newey's final years at Red Bull have been nothing short of historic. The cars he designed have not only won races but have also redefined the sport, pushing the boundaries of what was thought possible in Formula One engineering.

His departure comes at a time when Red Bull Racing has secured consecutive constructors' championships and has helped Max Verstappen become a three-time world champion.

The significance of Newey's final lap is underscored by the anticipation and speculation surrounding his next move. As Formula One prepares for a change in regulations beginning in 2026, Newey's expertise becomes the most prized commodity in the paddock.

Teams are lining up, eager to secure the services of a man whose designs have won more than 200 grands prix and who has been instrumental in achieving more than a dozen world championships.

Newey's final lap at Red Bull Racing is not just a farewell tour; it is a victory lap for a career that has been defined by an unyielding dedication to excellence. As he prepares to leave the team, the F1 world watches with bated breath, knowing that wherever he goes, innovation and success are sure to follow.

ADRIAN NEWEY HISTORY

DECISION TO LEAVE RED BULL RACING

Adrian Newey's decision to leave Red Bull Racing is a momentous shift in the Formula One landscape, akin to a grandmaster stepping away from the chessboard at the height of their powers.

His departure, set for the first quarter of 2025, marks the end of an epoch-making tenure with the team, during which he has been the architect behind a staggering array of victories and championship titles.

Newey's exit from Red Bull Racing is not a retreat but a transition to new challenges. He will pivot his focus to the final development and delivery of Red Bull's first hypercar, the RB17, a project that promises to encapsulate his design ethos in a vehicle that transcends the racetrack.

ADRIAN NEWEY HISTORY

This move is a testament to his relentless pursuit of engineering excellence, a pursuit that now seeks to conquer new realms beyond the world of Formula One.

The announcement of his departure was met with a mixture of surprise and anticipation. Newey's influence on the team and the sport has been so profound that his decision to step back from Formula One design duties has been likened to a seismic event.

His legacy at Red Bull Racing is unparalleled, having played a pivotal role in the team's ascension from an upstart newcomer to a titan of the sport, amassing an impressive seven F1 Drivers' and six Constructors' Championship titles.

The reasons behind Newey's decision are multifaceted. While he has expressed a desire to seek new challenges, there is also speculation about internal dynamics within the team and the allure of potential opportunities with other teams, such as Ferrari, which is undergoing a period of rebuilding and transformation.

The prospect of working with a team like Ferrari, especially alongside a driver of Lewis Hamilton's calibre, presents a new horizon for Newey to explore and perhaps conquer.

In the wake of his announcement, the F1 world is abuzz with speculation about the future. Newey's departure may prompt a brain drain from Red Bull, leaving a void that will be challenging to fill.

His decision has been met with respect and admiration, as well as a keen sense of anticipation for what the next chapter holds for a man who has been a defining force in the sport for nearly two decades.

As the final lap of Newey's career at Red Bull Racing approaches, the F1 community watches with bated breath, knowing that the end of this chapter is not the end of the story.

It is, instead, the beginning of a new narrative, one that will see Newey's genius applied to new ventures, continuing to push the boundaries of automotive engineering and design.

LEGACY AND IMPACT ON THE FUTURE OF FORMULA ONE.

Adrian Newey's legacy in Formula One is a tapestry of innovation, woven with the threads of his groundbreaking designs that have redefined the sport's landscape. His departure from Red Bull Racing in early 2025 is not just the turning of a page; it is the closing of a significant chapter in the annals of Formula One history.

Newey's impact on the future of Formula One is indelible. As the sport stands on the cusp of a new era, with significant regulatory changes on the horizon, his influence persists.

ADRIAN NEWEY HISTORY

The cars that have emerged from his drawing board have not only clinched championships but have also pushed the boundaries of automotive engineering, inspiring a generation of designers and engineers.

The cars designed by Newey are more than just vehicles; they are the embodiment of a philosophy that marries form with function, speed with safety, and aesthetics with aerodynamics.

His approach to car design has always been holistic, considering every aspect of the vehicle's performance. This philosophy will continue to influence how teams approach car design, even in his absence.

Newey's legacy is also evident in the way Formula One regards safety. The tragic death of Ayrton Senna, in a car designed by Newey, led to a renewed focus on driver safety, a legacy that continues to evolve and protect drivers in the sport.

ADRIAN NEWEY HISTORY

His designs have not only won races but have also contributed to making the sport safer for those behind the wheel.

As Formula One gears up for the transition to hybrid engines and a greater emphasis on aerodynamics, Newey's advocacy for advanced aerodynamics in future designs remains relevant. His vision for the crossover impact of F1 technology on road cars is a testament to his forward-thinking approach.

In essence, Adrian Newey's departure from Red Bull Racing is a momentous event, but his influence will continue to reverberate through the sport. His designs have set a benchmark for excellence, and his legacy will inspire future innovations in Formula One for years to come.

CHAPTER TEN

REFLECTIONS AND FUTURE HORIZONS

Adrian Newey's reflections on his storied career and his gaze toward future horizons are as intricate and forward-thinking as the Formula One cars he has designed.

As he prepares to depart from Red Bull Racing, a team he has been with for nearly two decades, Newey contemplates a legacy of innovation and success that is unparalleled in the sport's history.

His future, while not set in stone, is the subject of much speculation and interest. The prospect of joining Ferrari, a team undergoing a period of transformation and eager to return to championship glory, presents a new challenge for Newey.

It is an opportunity to work with Lewis Hamilton, a driver he has expressed admiration for, and to potentially add to his already impressive tally of achievements.

Newey's reflections are not just on his past successes but also on the potential for new beginnings. His departure from Red Bull Racing is not an end but a transition to a new chapter, one that may see him apply his design philosophy to new teams and new challenges.

The future horizons for Newey are vast, and the Formula One community watches with anticipation as one of its greatest minds contemplates his next move.

As the sport prepares for significant changes in regulations, Newey's expertise becomes even more valuable.

His ability to interpret and capitalise on new rules has been proven time and again, and his insights will be crucial for any team looking to gain a competitive edge in the coming seasons.

In his reflections, Newey may ponder the impact he has had on the sport, the advancements in safety he has championed, and the technological innovations he has introduced.

But it is the future horizons that hold the most promise, the opportunity to continue shaping the world of motorsport, and perhaps beyond, with his visionary approach to engineering and design.

NEWEY'S OWN REFLECTIONS ON HIS CAREER

Adrian Newey, a titan of Formula 1 engineering, has often shared his contemplations on a career that has shaped the very fabric of motorsport. His journey, marked by a relentless pursuit of aerodynamic perfection, is a testament to a life dedicated to the art and science of racing.

In the quiet moments away from the roar of engines and the bustle of the pit lanes, Newey has reflected on the paths he's taken and the roads not travelled. He has spoken of the allure of challenges unmet, notably his decision to remain with Red Bull Racing despite overtures from teams like Ferrari.

These choices, while leading to unparalleled success, also came with the wistful wonder of what might have been had he ventured into the storied garages of Maranello.

Newey's designs have not just won races; they have rewritten the annals of Formula 1 history. The Red Bull Racing RB19, for instance, stands as a monument to his genius, dominating the circuit with a staggering win rate.

Yet, even as he crafted machines that touched the pinnacle of performance, Newey has maintained a humility, a recognition of the ephemeral nature of success in a sport that is ever-evolving.

ADRIAN NEWEY HISTORY

As he approached the twilight of his tenure at Red Bull, Newey mused on the finite nature of his career. He acknowledged the countdown, the inexorable march of time that brings even the most illustrious careers to their denouement.

But rather than a lament, this acknowledgment seemed to fuel his passion further, driving him to pour his soul into the RB17 hypercar project before his eventual departure from the team.

Newey's reflections are not just musings on a personal odyssey; they are insights into the heart of innovation.

His career, punctuated by both triumphs and missed opportunities, offers a window into the mind of a man for whom the quest for speed transcends the mere mechanics of car design it is an expression of human aspiration, a dance with the limits of physics, and a romance with the very concept of victory.

In his own words, Newey has often conveyed a sense of gratitude for a life spent doing what he loves. His career, while marked by the inevitable passage of time, remains a beacon for those who dream of leaving their mark on the world of Formula 1. It is a narrative of passion, perseverance, and the unyielding desire to push beyond the boundaries of possibility.

THE RB17 HYPERCAR PROJECT AND FUTURE ENDEAVOURS

Adrian Newey's career, a tapestry of innovation and triumph, is entering a thrilling new chapter with the RB17 hypercar project. This endeavour is not merely a continuation of his legacy; it is a bold leap into a realm where the boundaries between automotive engineering and artistry blur into one.

The RB17 hypercar, a brainchild of Newey's visionary mind, is poised to redefine the limits of track performance.

ADRIAN NEWEY HISTORY

Conceived within the hallowed halls of Red Bull Advanced Technologies, this machine is the culmination of decades of Formula 1 mastery, distilled into a two-seat marvel of speed and sophistication.

With only 50 units slated for production, the RB17 is as exclusive as it is revolutionary, a testament to Newey's relentless pursuit of perfection.

As Newey prepares to bid farewell to his storied tenure at Red Bull Racing, the RB17 stands as his parting gift, a hypercar that promises over 1,100 horsepower wrapped in a carbon-composite chassis, embodying the most advanced ground effect package ever seen in a production car.

It is a vehicle that does not merely exist within the confines of what is known but dares to venture into the uncharted territories of automotive potential.

Beyond the RB17, the future is a canvas of possibilities for Newey. Speculation abounds regarding his next steps, with whispers of interest from the most storied teams in Formula 1.

The allure of working with legendary drivers and the chance to once again redefine the sport's landscape may beckon. Yet, whatever path he chooses, it is certain that Newey's influence will continue to reverberate through the corridors of motorsport history.

Newey's reflections on his career thus far reveal a man who views his work not as a series of achievements but as a continuous journey of exploration and discovery. The RB17 hypercar project is not the final chapter but a gateway to future endeavours that will undoubtedly bear the hallmark of his genius. For Adrian Newey, the race is never over; it is simply the beginning of the next exhilarating lap.

EPILOGUE

THE AUTHOR'S CLOSING THOUGHTS ON ADRIAN NEWEY'S LIFE AND CAREER.

Adrian Newey's life and career unfold like a grand tapestry, woven with threads of innovation, determination, and an unquenchable thirst for speed. His story is not merely one of technical triumphs; it is a narrative that captures the essence of human endeavour in the face of relentless competition.

The legacy of Newey is etched into the very chassis of Formula 1 history. His designs have not only crossed finish lines but have also redrawn them, pushing the sport into new eras of performance and possibility.

ADRIAN NEWEY HISTORY

The cars that sprang from his drafting table are more than mere vehicles; they are vessels of dreams, carrying the aspirations of drivers and the spirits of teams to glory.

As Newey transitions from the adrenaline-fueled world of Formula 1 to the meticulous crafting of the RB17 hypercar, his reflections on a storied career reveal a man who has always looked beyond the horizon. The RB17 is not an end but a beacon, signalling his ongoing quest to merge the realms of art and engineering.

The departure of Newey from Red Bull Racing marks the end of an era, but not the cessation of his influence. His departure is set to take place in the first quarter of 2025, leaving behind a legacy that will continue to inspire and challenge the norms of automotive design.

ADRIAN NEWEY HISTORY

The RB19, his most dominant Formula One car, winning 21 out of the 22 races it competed in, stands as a testament to his unparalleled skill.

In the quiet reflection of his achievements, Newey has often spoken of the collaborative nature of his success, the symphony of minds and hands that brought his visions to life.

His career is a reminder that behind every great innovation lies a team, a family of professionals driven by a shared passion for excellence.

As the pages of Newey's career turn, one cannot help but feel a sense of anticipation for what is yet to come. The future endeavours of this engineering maestro are shrouded in potential, each possibility more exciting than the last.

Wherever his journey takes him, the impact of Adrian Newey's life and career will resonate through the annals of motorsport for generations to come. It is a legacy built not on laurels rested upon but on the continuous pursuit of that which lies just out of reach, always driving forward, always racing against the best opponent of all – the relentless march of time and technology.

CONCLUSION

LIST OF FORMULA ONE CHAMPIONSHIPS.

Adrian Newey's storied career in Formula One is a chronicle of relentless innovation and success. His designs have not merely competed but have consistently set the standard for excellence in the pinnacle of motorsport. The list of Formula One Championships won by teams under his technical wizardry is a testament to his enduring genius.

Newey's creations have clinched **twelve Constructors' Championships** across three different teams. These mechanical marvels have also propelled seven different drivers to win **thirteen Drivers' Championships**.

His tenure at Williams, McLaren, and Red Bull Racing has been marked by a series of dominant cars that have left an indelible mark on the sport.

ADRIAN NEWEY HISTORY

The cars designed by Newey have been more than just vehicles; they have been the chariots of champions, the dreams of drivers made manifest in carbon fibre and metal. Each championship won is a chapter in the epic saga of a man whose life's work has been dedicated to the pursuit of speed and the art of the possible.

The Newey-designed Red Bull Racing RB19, in particular, stands as a colossus among Formula One cars, with an astonishing victory in 21 out of the 22 races it competed in.

This level of dominance is unparalleled, a clear reflection of Newey's ability to blend aerodynamic efficiency with mechanical performance.

As the sun sets on Newey's active involvement in Formula One design, with his focus shifting to the RB17 hypercar project, the racing world watches with bated breath.

ADRIAN NEWEY HISTORY

His departure from day-to-day duties at Red Bull Racing is set for the first quarter of 2025, marking the end of an era. Yet, the legacy of the championships won under his guidance will continue to resonate through the sport for years to come.

In the annals of Formula One, Adrian Newey's name is written in bold, not just for the championships won but for the spirit of innovation he brought to the track.

His career is a beacon for all who dare to dream in the language of speed and for those who believe that the race is never truly over. It is a legacy of triumph, a symphony of engineering prowess that will echo through the ages.

ADRIAN NEWEY HISTORY

24 HOURS OF LE MANS RESULTS.

Adrian Newey's foray into the 24 Hours of Le Mans is a lesser-known chapter of his illustrious career, yet it is one that offers a glimpse into his passion for motorsport beyond the Formula One circuits. While Newey is celebrated for his F1 triumphs, his involvement in Le Mans speaks to a broader ambition: to conquer the varied terrains of automotive racing.

The 24 Hours of Le Mans, a crucible of endurance and engineering, presents a unique challenge that Newey could not resist. It is a race that tests not only the speed but the stamina of both car and driver, a marathon dance with time and technology.
In this arena, Newey's contributions have been more personal, a testament to his love for the raw, unfiltered essence of racing.

Newey's engagement with Le Mans has been multifaceted, from providing technical insights to actively participating in the event. His role may not have been front and centre as in Formula One, but his impact was no less significant.

The cars that bore the touch of his genius at Le Mans were imbued with the same relentless pursuit of aerodynamic perfection that marked his F1 designs.

While the records may not show a string of victories akin to his F1 legacy, Newey's Le Mans results are not to be measured in podium finishes alone. They are to be found in the silent hours of the night, on the long stretches of the Mulsanne Straight, where the spirit of his engineering prowess raced against the ticking clock, pushing the limits of endurance racing.

In the grand narrative of Adrian Newey's career, Le Mans stands as a bold statement of his versatility and his undying quest for racing excellence. It is a chapter that may not dominate the headlines but one that offers a profound insight into the man whose life has been a symphony of speed, a relentless pursuit of victory in the face of the most daunting challenges motorsport has to offer.

Made in the USA
Columbia, SC
16 October 2024